Things That Go
FIND IT! COLOR IT!

Diana Zourelias

DOVER PUBLICATIONS, INC.
MINEOLA, NEW YORK

Put on your detective hat and see if you can find the image that doesn't belong among the other things on each page. Be on the lookout for cleverly hidden modes of transportation, including an ambulance, bicycle, cruise ship, hot air balloon, taxi, tractor, and even a skateboard! If you can't seem to spot one of the hidden "moving" vehicles, solutions are provided at the end of the book, following plate 29. For added fun, color each of the amusing illustrations with crayons or colored pencils. The cover image with the answer shown is an example of the activities included inside this book.

Bibliographical Note

Things That Go: Find It! Color It! is a new work, first published by
Dover Publications, Inc., in 2017.

International Standard Book Number
ISBN-13: 978-0-486-81383-7
ISBN-10: 0-486-81383-5

Manufactured in the United States by LSC Communications
81383501   2017
www.doverpublications.com

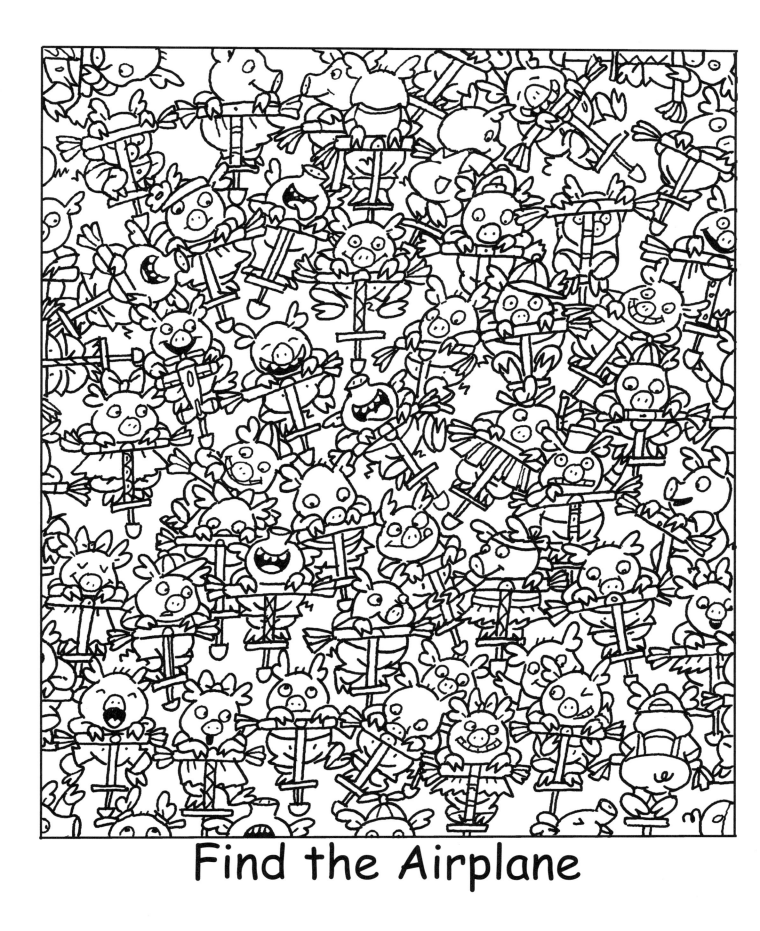

Find the Airplane

Find the Ambulance

Find the Bicycle

Find the Blimp

Find the Bus

Find the Car

Find the Cement Truck

Find the Cruise Ship

Find the Dump Truck

Find the Fire Truck

Find the Helicopter

Find the Hot Air Balloon

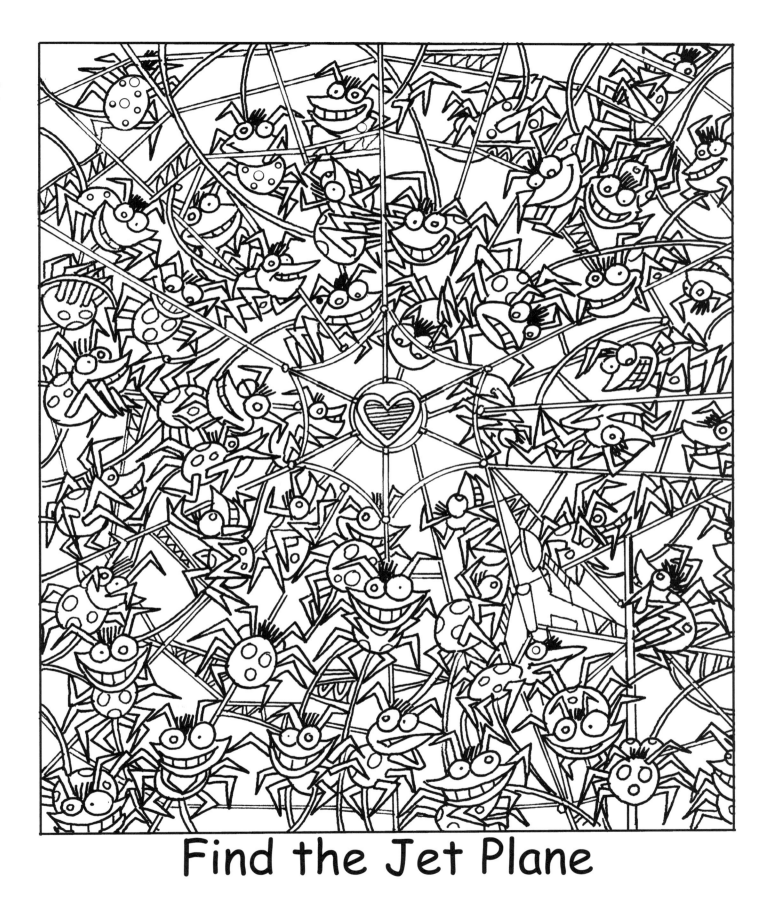

Find the Jet Plane

Find the Mail Truck

Find the Motor Boat

Find the Motorcycle

Find the Race Car

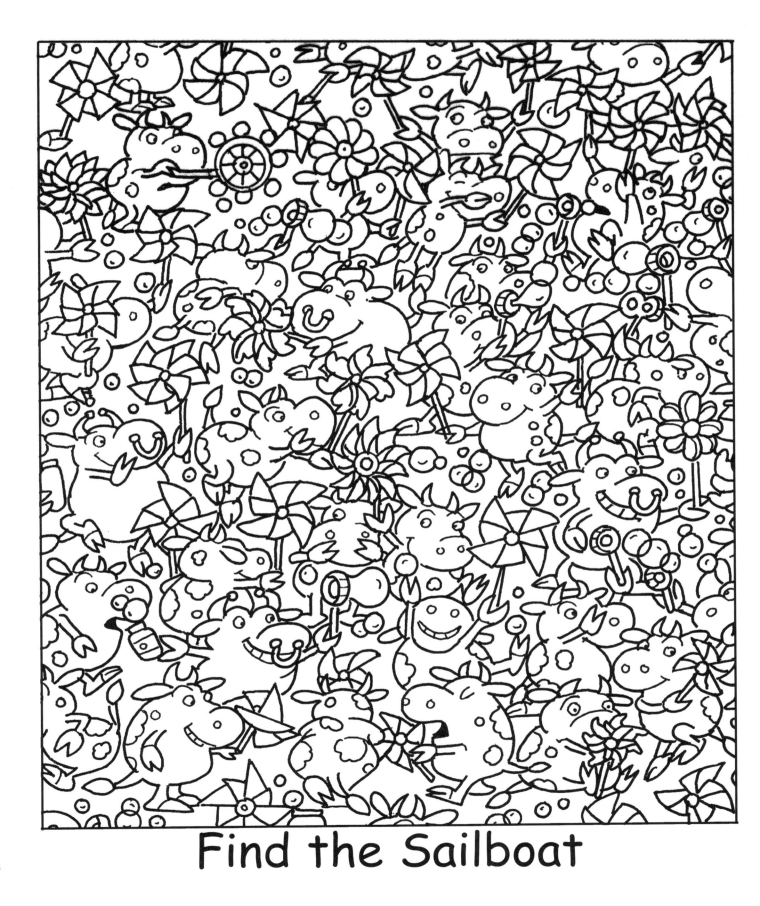

Find the Sailboat

Find the Scooter

Find the Seaplane

Find the Skateboard

Find the Space Shuttle

Find the Submarine

Find the Tank

Find the Taxi

Find the Tow Truck

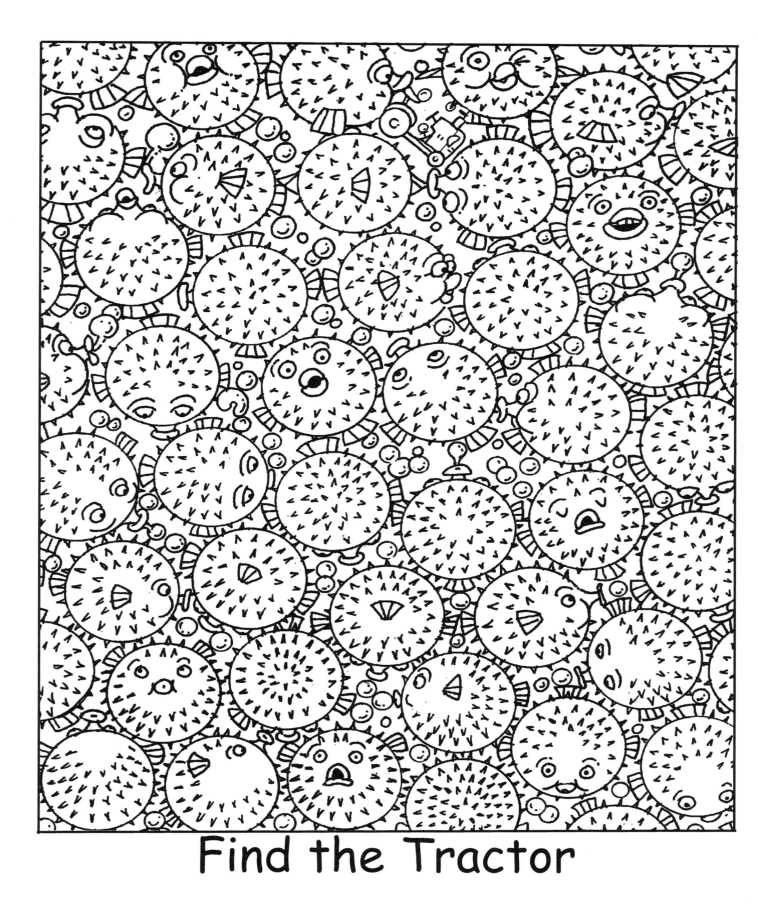

Find the Tractor

Find the Train Engine

Find the Tugboat

SOLUTIONS

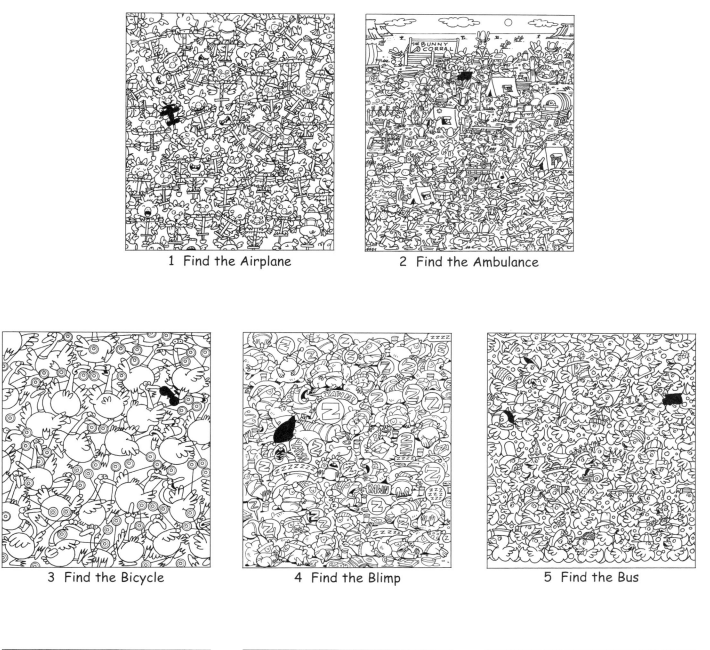

1 Find the Airplane

2 Find the Ambulance

3 Find the Bicycle

4 Find the Blimp

5 Find the Bus

6 Find the Car

7 Find the Cement Truck

8 Find the Cruise Ship

9 Find the Dump Truck

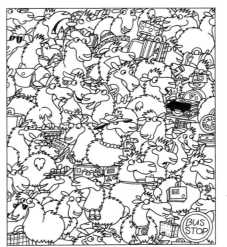

10 Find the Fire Truck

11 Find the Helicopter

12 Find the Hot Air Balloon

13 Find the Jet Plane

14 Find the Mail Truck

15 Find the Motor Boat

16 Find the Motorcycle

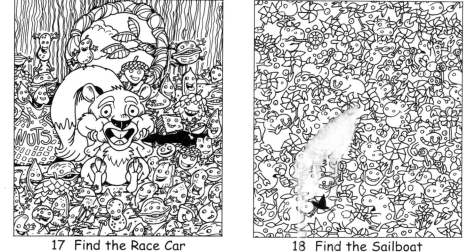

17 Find the Race Car

18 Find the Sailboat

19 Find the Scooter

20 Find the Seaplane

21 Find the Skateboard

22 Find the Space Shuttle

23 Find the Submarine

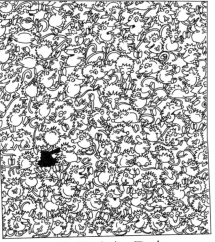

24 Find the Tank

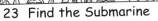

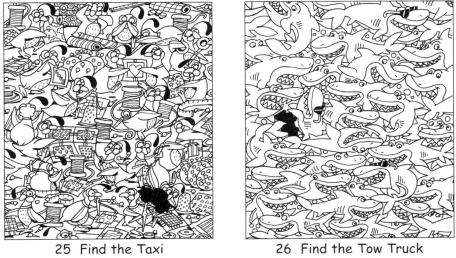

25 Find the Taxi

26 Find the Tow Truck

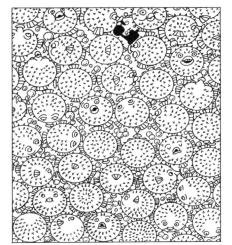

27 Find the Tractor

28 Find the Train Engine

29 Find the Tugboat